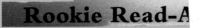
Rookie Read-A

D0427823

Recycle That!

By Fay Robinson

Consultants

Robert L. Hillerich, Professor Emeritus,
Bowling Green State University, Bowling Green, Ohio;
Consultant, Pinellas County Schools, Florida

Lynne Kepler, Educational Consultant

CHILDRENS PRESS®

CHICAGO

Design by Herman Adler Design Group
Photo Research by Feldman & Associates, Inc.

Library of Congress Cataloging-in-Publication Data

Robinson, Fay.
    Recycle that! / by Fay Robinson.
        p. cm. – (Rookie read-about science)
    ISBN 0-516-06033-3
        1. Recycling (Waste, etc.)—Juvenile literature. [1. Recycling
    (Waste)] I. Title. II. Series.
TD794.5.R634   1995
363.72'82–dc20   94-35626
                                                        CIP
                                                        AC

Bottles, cans, mail, magazines, boxes, bags . . . We throw out a lot of trash!

Everything we throw away
came from somewhere.
The paper products we use
— newspaper, magazines,
cards, boxes — are made
from trees.

Thousands and thousands of trees are cut down each day to make the paper we use.

Fields and hills are dug up
to get sand to make glass,
and metals to make cans.

The plastics we use are
made with oil pumped
from deep inside the earth.

Each time we take
something from the
earth, we change the earth.

The ways we change it are
not always good for us, or
for wild animals.

And where does all our
trash go?

Most of it goes into
landfills — large areas
of land set aside just for
trash. But we throw out
so much trash that our
landfills are filling up.
Soon there won't be
any more room!

By using and throwing
away so many things,
we have created a big
problem. What can
you do to help?
Recycle!

When something is
recycled, all or part
of it is used again.

Many towns and cities have special programs for recycling. Each home gets a special container for items to be recycled.

Often, cans, bottles, and newspapers can be recycled. In some places, magazines and plastic bottles can be recycled, too.

A recycling truck comes
to pick up the recyclables.
Each material goes into
its own bin.

The truck driver drives
to a recycling center,

where everything is sorted and bundled.

People also bring things
to the recycling center
themselves. In places where
there is no pick-up service,
this is the only way to recycle.

Every few days, trucks
come to the recycling
center to take each
material to factories . . .

where old glass can be
made into new glass,

old cans can be made
into new cans,

old paper can be made
into new paper,

and old plastics can be made into new plastic items — like this playground equipment.

You can also recycle by reusing things — like bags, boxes, and plastic bottles.

Can you see why it's smart to recycle? Things that would have been wasted can be made into something useful instead!

Each time you recycle
one can, bottle, or
newspaper, you help
the earth a little bit.
So recycle that! It's easy!

Words You Know

recycling center

landfill

glass

plastics

paper products

recycling containers

recycling truck

Index

About the Author

Fay Robinson is an early childhood specialist who lives and works in the Chicago area. She received a bachelor's degree in Child Study from Tufts University and a master's degree in Education from Northwestern University. She has taught preschool and elementary children and is the author of several picture books.

Photo Credits

©Cameramann International, Ltd. – 13, 30 (bottom)

PhotoEdit – ©Robert Brenner, 3, 23, 31 (top left); ©Alan Oddie, 10; ©Tony Freeman, 25, 26, 28

Photri – 18, 31 (bottom)

SuperStock International, Inc. – ©Scott Barrow, Cover; ©Richard Heinzen, 7; ©Mia & Klaus Matthes, 9; ©John Warden, 17; ©Roger Lee, 19, 30 (top); ©Charles Orrico, 20, 24, 31 (top right); ©David Forbert, 21, 31 (center right)

Unicorn Stock Photos – ©Jim Shippee, 8, 22; ©Jeff Greenberg, 14; ©Tom McCarthy, 16; ©Karen Holsinger Mullen, 27; ©Charles E. Schmidt, 29

Valan – ©Val Wilkinson, 4, 31 (center left)

COVER: Recycling bin